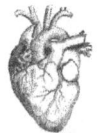

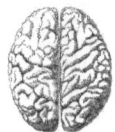

TO BREAK THE HEART OF THE SUN

William Taylor Jr.

WORDS DANCE PUBLISHING
WordsDance.com

1st Edition
ISBN-13: 978-0692617380
ISBN-10: 0692617388

Cover design & interior layout by Amanda Oaks

Type set in Bergamo, Alfa Slab One, Langdon, Archivo Black

Words Dance Publishing
WordsDance.com

For John Panzer

TO BREAK THE HEART OF THE SUN
William Taylor Jr.

TO BREAK THE HEART OF THE SUN

THE PLACE WHERE REAL MUSIC IS BORN

She said, baby, I'm as sad as fuck,

and I said, honey, that's just the way
some of us are born;

it's our gift, our lifestyle.

Those other folks, they never really learn
how to sing,

they've never been to the place
where real music is born.

They've never knocked back the sorrow of the years
like a cheap wine and chased it
with a shot of something
beautiful and lost

while listening to the secrets
the moon tells
when it's too drunk
to know what it is.

When the big darkness finally comes to claim us
and the world blooms with the truth of it

those other folks will be lost and frightened,
they'll curse their gods and everything else
they bought,
but you and me, we'll get our tickets punched
and stride right into the heart of it
like it was our living room.

BASEBALL

It's late October in the Tenderloin,
and no one here could tell you
what holds the world
together or why,
but the Giants made the series,
and it's tied up, 2 games to 2,
so that'll have to do for now.
Most of us don't need much
to get us through the days–
dime bags of hope
to keep us going until the next whatever.
Most of my neighborhood
is crushed into bars, yelling
at television screens
for justice,
and I'm waiting in line
at the corner store to buy my beer.
The fellow in front of me
is buying ticket after ticket,
furiously scratching at them with a dirty quarter,
wheezing and cursing as if his life
depended on winning, and maybe it did,
but when he ran out of dollars
the counter and the floor were littered
with his failure.
He stormed into the street
like a demon, damning the universe and everybody.
I get my beer and drink it
on the steps of my building
and the woman pacing in front of the laundromat
across the street is gesturing wildly and talking to the air.
She looks pretty in her tattered pink dress
but when she comes over to ask
for five dollars and a cigarette
I tell her I have neither.
She sneers with a toothless rage
as the man from the liquor store

passes out in a nearby doorway
and the schizophrenic guy from apartment four
starts a knife fight with a Post St. pimp
named Eddy.
I take my beer inside,
the toothless woman telling me where I can shove it.
Minutes later I peek through the blinds
and the schizophrenic guy is on his back
in a puddle of blood,
but there's still a chance the Giants
could pull it of in the 9th.

SUNDAY AFTERNOON AT THE BROWN JUG

We're sitting at the bar and Janey's crying in her drink,
slobbering really, telling me a story I can't
understand, something about a man who
loved her and is no longer here.

On the TV above the bar there's a docudrama
about the Irish Mafia in New York

while outside a woman with a mangy dog
wanders the sidewalk calling a name
with the voice of someone lost in a forest
on a night without stars.

"Pop! Right in the head!"
a patron yells at the TV screen
as a hapless informant meets his end.

Outside there's still three hours of daylight
and no one knows what to do with them.

A PORTRAIT OF BAUDELAIRE

It's Sunday afternoon and that's better than a lot of things.
I'm at Vesuvio drinking beer
and crushing on the pretty waitress.

There's a portrait of Baudelaire on the wall
above my table and he frowns down upon me
with a lonely disdain.

I can see his sad heart shining
through his chest and I guess I'm much the same.

He says, if you would not feel
the horrible burden of time
forever crushing you to the earth,

you must always be drunk!

I tell him I'm doing the best I can,

currently intoxicated with wine,
sunlight
and the pretty waitress with my drinks.

Down in Kerouac Alley there's the gentleman with the tie
who stands all day trying to sell newspapers
to the tourists and the pretty girls
who summarily ignore him
but he never seems to mind.

I glance down from my upstairs seat
by the window and he waves and smiles
and I wave and smile,
and we seem to share a secret understanding
about what exactly, I couldn't say.

When I leave I give him

all the dollars in my pocket
like I do most every Sunday

and he smiles and I smile,
and I wish drunkenness
on the both of us

as I make my way home
through Chinatown crowds,
every face some kind of prayer.

THIS BURNING MOMENT

I walk the streets of this
city of poets

and see them everywhere I go

they're not hard to recognize

they're in the crowded cafès
and poorly lit bars

taking strange pills
drinking bad wine

pushing blades
and needles to their
too sensitive skin

crawling through the alleys of Chinatown
jumping off downtown roofs

in and out of psych wards
and hospitals

fighting amongst themselves

selling peanuts at ball games
to try and make the rent

they know nothing of the past
or the future just

this burning moment

their laughter is true

and sometimes they laugh
as they burn

and sometimes they scream

but their ashes are
always beautiful.

THE MOVEMENT OF YOUR HANDS

And if you live long enough
there is a grief that will find you
in one form or another;
a grief that will break you,
a grief you won't recover from.
The rest of your life will be spent
in its aftermath.
You'll hide it as best you can
but it will be seen in your eyes
and heard in your manner
of speaking.
It will be obvious in the way you walk
and in the movement of your hands.
You'll live in fear
of, at any given moment,
collapsing
on a street corner
in broad daylight
beneath the weight of it,
the truth of it
spilling out from you
like blood,
forming puddles
on the sidewalk
for the people
to step over
on their way
to something else.

A SINGLE SONG

I stand at the corner of Columbus and Broadway
and inside the Condor Club a local band
plays some tourist friendly
version of jazz

while across the street
a group of old Chinese men
sit upon the sidewalk
with traditional strings
making sad old music
from long ago

the cacophony fills the street
and blends together into a single song
carried down through the ages

I stand in the middle of it
listening
until the light changes

then continue on my way
as if there were somewhere
I was supposed to be.

PEOPLE WHO MEAN WELL

People who mean well,
they'll try and tell you things
like, do whatever it is
you are meant to do.

I imagine whatever these people
are meant to do lets them
sleep at night,
or at least pays the rent.

I guess they don't think much about
what happens if what you're meant to do
leaves you lost and broken in some
hotel on Geary Street,

half insane
in some tiny room,
too far gone to cry.

These same people will tell you things
like, life never gives you more
than you can handle,

while every day I step outside
into a world of people who were given
more than they can handle;

you can hear it in their voices,
you can see it in their eyes
and the way their hands shake.

Another thing people will tell you
is that death is necessary
in order to give meaning to life,

but I've yet to see a death

that's given meaning
to anything at all,

and if they really believed it
they wouldn't have invented god.

They can have their death.

Me, I could wake into this mess of beauty
and terror again and again, for eternity,

even though it's far more than I can handle
and I have no idea what I was meant to do.

HOW I SPEND ALL MY TIME

I want to go wherever it is
real music
is born

the place where the ancient sorrow of things
is the air in which you live
breathe
and drown

where joy
is a kind of madness
not reached by words

O I lived there for years

but at some point was cast out
with the rest of you

and now spend
all my time
trying to get
back there again

I feel it
inside me
like something asleep
and half-forgotten

a home even now
not completely lost to me

in dreams it still
knows my name

when I find it again
I'll let you know

you'll wake in darkness

your face wet with tears
and understand.

THE WORD

I have seen the faces
of the broken all my life
their eyes all faraway
and pleading
their faces like the victims
of unspeakable accidents
and I have always wondered how they lived
wondered what kept them
going
through the days like ghosts
no one wants to remember
and now that I am of them
I have come to understand
that like me
they are waiting for a word
from someone
who no longer loves them
a word with the power to save them
a word that deep down
they know will never come
and like me they imagine
they might one day
accept this
and somehow find it in them
to save themselves
and be worthy of love once more
but that day, should it come
is not this day
and for now
me and the
rest of the broken
we just
pass the hours
with our
confusion
and loss
waiting
and waiting
for a word.

BENEATH IT

It's the kind of night when all that's left
is the waiting for whatever it is that seeks us
to arrive.

We've squandered our luck
and burned through mercy,

your eyes shine like stars that died
before their light ever made it
anywhere.

The bones of our lovesongs
are bleached and broken
and washed up on dirty beaches,
strewn about the sidewalks
of neighborhoods we're afraid to go.

The music of things is muted
and should we try and sing
the neighbors would complain.

People will try and tell you things,
but there's not much that they know.

The moon's indifference
is a kind of mother,

offering a love
we'll never be equal to.

The hooker outside stands beneath it
and when I tell her I don't have a cigarette

she says,

It's just as well,
those things'll kill ya.

She spits and laughs like some
broken thing and says,

but then so will everything else.

THE HORN

The day isn't much,
another thing half-born
and destined for obscurity.

It's too hot.

The poems aren't coming
and the story just isn't
very good.

The sun gives in
and I don't know
what to do with anything.

I almost wish
I were back at work,
where I don't have to
flail about so much
for purpose or direction.

I just screw the one thing
onto the other,

and move on to the next,
again and again.

The hours pass,
empty but without much
trouble,

and then the horn
eventually sounds,
telling me I'm done.

ALL I AM ACCUSED OF

So I lie myself down in this shabby
bed I've made, my ragged pockets
overflowing with crazy luck and unexpected joy;
my weak heart swelling, in spite of everything,
with laughter that shakes my brittle bones.
And it's true, I'm guilty of all I'm accused of
and more, but so are you, so are you,
but I'm willing to forgive the both of us, even
if you're not. See, I just want the general and ongoing
horror of things to grant me pardon for a little while more,
because my love still outweighs my bitterness
and I still laugh and love with all
my blasted being, in spite of cops and judges
and the sad old businessmen in this
sad old bar, and I am shameless in my joy,
offering up tiny prayers to anyone who'll
listen, and listen, right now my heart is so many
shades of blue you'd surely blush
to see it.

THE DREAMS AND PRAYERS OF THE WORLD

The world is just another trap
when there's nothing in particular
you want to be

your soul a mess of unfinished books

your face a map
of lost things

we wander the city
and marvel
how no one cares
that all the cars
and all the buildings are ugly

and there's nothing we can do
for the dead pigeons
on the sidewalk
or the ones in our hearts

and there's that woman
who wanders Post St.
cursing to herself in smeared lipstick
and when you look in her eyes
you can see the place
where all the dreams and prayers of the world
are caught and torn
on the barbed wire fence
that keeps us from whatever heaven
is or isn't there

hard-eyed girls on skateboards
fly past

as a shirtless man with sad tattoos
screams at a skinny girl
from a third story window

while we stand and smoke
beneath the dying sun
like banished gods
waiting
for our turn at burning.

IN MY VEINS LIKE A FIRE

I guess the best way to explain it
is to imagine the perfect and irrefutable
sorrow of the world
that lies at the core of everything

and me digging for it
like some forgotten prisoner
with a broken spoon

a curious undertaking to be sure

sorrow knows our names
and writes our dreams
we've no reason
to seek it out

and yet to somehow take it unawares
to breach the very heart of it
and make its terrible secret
my own

is the dream that drags me onward

see, sometimes
when I feel it in my veins
like a fire

when I speak with its voice
and see with its eyes

I know I am closer to something.

THE SMALL THINGS

She says the small things aren't enough,

says all the precious moments
are just baubles collecting dust,

the poets tattered scarecrows
in abandoned fields
splintered by the wind.

We are of no use to one another,

deformed by our own
separate hells,

staring across chasms,
the bridges all in flames.

TO HEAR THE MUSIC

The poets are getting old
time was never
their friend
even in the best of days
the future a vague doom
stalking their dreams
the world beats the magic
out of most everyone eventually
and while the sane and the practical
were doing what they could
to make it through the days intact
the fool poets were listening to the music
of the universe
and trying to write it down
for all of those who couldn't hear
but the world never much cared for such things
and now the poets are getting old
selling hot dogs on Market street
to make rent
they're driving cabs
busing tables at Specs
in exchange for drinks
working at toy stores
and sandwich shops, any place
that will have them
they're sitting in their little
Tenderloin apartments right now
drinking their last beer waiting
to be evicted
they're crying in their sleep
having sloppy affairs
still listening to that funny music
in their heads, they've never
been good for much else
and they hardly ever bother
to write it down anymore
they'd rather spend their time

sitting in plastic chairs
outside North Beach cafès
nursing their wine
watching the girls
feeling the sun upon their face
while they can
and they start to disappear one by one
maybe you'll see a little something
in the paper
about how one of them died
in his little apartment
and another on the BART train
on the way back from Oakland
and another jumped
or maybe fell from a bridge
alone, always
alone, and you might
think it sad as you shake your head
and maybe so
but you weren't there to hear the music.

ALWAYS THE SUN

Today a letter informs me
the collection agency is suing for
six thousand dollars
I do not have.

And then
there's a phone call to say
a friend from long ago
is gone by cancer.

I study his photograph
and it feels like a warning,
a harbinger of things to come.

Death has a hat the size of the sun
holding all our names.

I step outside and the landlord says it's such
a beautiful day, and I walk
past beautiful women
laughing at sidewalk tables
and stinking men asleep in doorways.

Everywhere love is stretched
as thin as a thread
and the sun, always the sun,
glorious and terrible,
shining down so
indifferent upon it all.

And the only thing I can think to hope
is that at the end of it
we'll have stored up enough joy
to balance out the darkness.

It's the only victory I can still imagine.

ME AND THE HEART

for David Lerner

Over the years
me and the heart
we've had some crazy times
gone strange places
both good and bad
seen and done some questionable things
but like any true poet
like any lost soul
I've always trusted the heart
no questions asked
but lately the heart's been taking me
to strange neighborhoods
I never knew existed
places not on any map
I've ever seen
last week we drove for days
on an unknown highway
and eventually found ourselves
in a dead-end alley beneath an unfamiliar sky
the stars and the moon had called off sick
and the next thing I knew
beauty in the form
of a dark girl's laughter
came out of nowhere
like a common thug
it was upon me
remorseless it took me apart
like the amateur I was
left me on my knees
broken and ashamed
in a puddle of my own blood
and tears
before disappearing back into darkness
swearing I'd never
see it again
not even if I begged

all the while the heart just stood and watched
and in misery I looked to it
for some kind of answer some kind of
explanation for its treachery
and the heart just sneered
mocking and pitiless
telling me I knew very well
where we'd end up
sooner or later
and to not be such a baby about it
the heart told me to pull my sad ass up off the ground
brush it off
wipe my stupid nose and get back
into the goddamned car
cos it was getting late
and we were only halfway there.

WHAT THE FEAR TELLS ME

The great animal fear of the world
is what stays with us,
is what our bones are made of.

Love burns off in the sun,
strength gives way,
anything you can name
slips through your shaking hands.

The fear sleeps, but it's never far
from the surface of things.
Those who say otherwise
are liars and always running.

God's an empty bottle
in the face of it,
whatever you've constructed
to keep it at bay
gives like splintered wood.

It's a fine afternoon;
there's wine and sunlight,
pretty girls beneath it.

But the fear is there in every shadow.

I drink beer to try and keep it quiet,
I offer these words
as a kind of appeasement,

but it's in me like a heart.

I dearly want to call
and explain these things,
because I think you'd
understand,

but the fear tells me

you won't pick up,

and it's probably right;
just like when it says

I should have listened to my father,

and how I'll never find
a good ending
for this poem.

TO BREAK THE HEART OF THE SUN

for John Panzer

Maybe you just wanted some attention,
maybe you were just bored
and wanted to see what everyone
was so frightened of,
when you sought out the dark.
Maybe you just wanted to see
what it was made of,
where it could take you.
You learned to speak its language
and sing with its voice;
the dark taught you a new kind of laughter
and gave you knowledge the light never could.
You wore it like a favorite shirt,
like a pair of fancy shoes,
you wore it like a crow's wings
and flew to places you'd only
read about in books.
You wore it like a mask
until its face became your own.
You took the dark inside you like a second heart,
until you ceased to exist as a separate thing.
Yet sometimes you remembered the light
with an aching fondness,
on moonless nights you dreamed
of it like you would an old lover.
But the dark is a jealous thing
and holds you like a mother.
So you waited for a moment
when the dark
was otherwise engaged
and you scrambled back to the light like a thief,
the dark clinging to you like fire,
you and your stories to break
the heart of the sun.
You stood beneath it, naked
with blinking eyes,

cursed and beautiful,
the dark inside you burning
with a terrible light,
and the people didn't know
whether to stare
or look away.

AS WE WAIT FOR THE MOMENT WHEN I DISAPPOINT YOU

We both know it's coming as sure as the dawn
but for now let's put it in the place
where we keep all the things
we don't think about
until we have to.

It's a lovely afternoon
and we've found a pretty good place
to hide

and seeing my face
from a certain angle
and in a certain light

it's possible to imagine
that this thing between us
has transformed me into something
bigger than I am.

And it's true that sometimes people
have been known
to rise above their baser selves
to forge the future like a spear

and for now it's much more pleasant
to think of that
rather than the other

because this thing inside me
could be mistaken for love

the sex is good

and sometimes it's fun
to believe in things.

THE BURNING MOON AND THE CRIES OF OWLS

for John Swain

Each day we wake into the terrible
fire of our lives,
and much of us aches
to dissolve into the great
and wondrous sorrow of it.
But at the core of our hearts
lies a wild joy at the burning;
it pulls us like puppets
to any number of silly dooms,
and though sometimes we find
a temporary peace,
some awkward haven in which
to rest awhile,
our shadow selves never let us
stay for long.
Soon enough something sings us
back into the night,
back beneath the burning moon
and the cries of owls
in search of some new trouble
to be equal to,
pausing now and then
beneath dead
and dying stars,
hunched with hands
of blood and parchment,
trying to translate fire
into words,
all the while understanding
our failure to be predestined,
utter
and glorious.

AT THE AMSTERDAM

The day is ashamed of itself
and wishes to be done

in its defense it never asked to be born
anymore than the rest of us

who are lost within it
dazed and drained of luck

arguing with gods
bargaining with demons

staggering across concrete
with animal eyes of fear and rage

and the eventual collapse of things
is the only bus that arrives on time

there's nothing I can save so I
have another beer at the Amsterdam

and watch a woman stand beneath the sun
as she smokes a cigarette and talks into a phone

like it all makes perfect sense and nothing is wrong.

CHAINS

I imagine the world, too,
is in chains, beholden
to ancient rules it never
agreed to or understood.

It grinds us down with jagged teeth
but I think mostly without malice,
like it once had other dreams.

At some point we are forced
to stand shivering
and naked before the things
we've thrown away,

the beauty abandoned
like something
that could be replaced.

I scour the night
for cut-rate demons
with which to bargain,
but I've only trinkets,
leftovers and common
forgeries to my name,

nothing I could exchange
for another night
beneath her eyes.

MY WEAK HEART NEVER ASKED TO BE BORN
BUT MOST DAYS IT DOES THE BEST IT CAN

The years beat down our rage
into a quiet sorrow.

People talk of the weather
and what they ate for lunch.

I drink beer in a quiet room
as outside the rain
falls down in a fine
and steady mist.

Today there is an emptiness
that touches everything

but I bear it no grudge.

Things fall apart
as they always have,
there's nothing new in this.

I breathe in
and out,

existing in the moment
and waiting for the next.

EVERYTHING THAT KILLS ME

The day is hot and dry
and I wait on poetry
like I wait on rain.

I walk out into it
hoping to find
whatever it is I'm
hungry for,

some splinter of mercy
abandoned somewhere
I forgot to look.

Like any American I am addicted
to all the things I can't afford,

in love with everything
that kills me.

The blue of the sky looks kind
and forgiving;

I do not trust it
but it is beautiful and beyond
my comprehension,

so I ask no questions
and follow where it leads.

WHATEVER'S LEFT OF THE DAY

I'm sorry, I mean, for the way things are,
for the sorrow like a hungry dog
that follows us home each night
and wanders our cobblestone dreams.
I'm sorry for the failure of love
and all the ways it breaks us
and the silence of these rooms,
empty and haunted by the ghosts
of our better selves,
and I hate the way everything we try and build
falls apart in our hands,
no matter how hard we try
and keep it.
I guess we're not strong enough,
good
or smart enough,
and I look at all the faces
in restaurants and bars and office buildings
and the tired stories they tell,
and I think how there should be
somebody in charge of this kind of thing,
I think whomever it was with the grand idea
to put the whole sad world into motion
needs to step up
and put it right or shut it down
or something.
I don't know if they're dead or drunk
or sleeping it off in some mystic alley,
or if they just moved along and left us here,
all unfinished and strange.
Maybe they're not any better
than the rest of us
and maybe we should try
and fix it ourselves,
but it's so much bigger than us,
and meaner.
We were just born into it,

all broken and frightened
and lost, and me, I'm not good
for much of anything
anymore,
I can't even fit together
whatever's left of the day.
I'm just saying somebody
should do something.

THE DEFEATED ARMIES OF RUINED AGES

The grand and pristine indifference of the universe
is the only lesson you really
need to learn
after that everything else
falls into place
and you'll come to realize
that your broken heart
is a one legged pigeon
or the story the junkie
tries to tell you
as she clings
to your arm
on any number of nights
you've long since
forgotten
you'll understand
the failure of your life
and all your wasted hours
are not unique
nor are they punishment
for sins in this
or any other world
think of the defeated armies
of ruined ages
think of dinosaurs
and dodos
your sister's stillborn dreams
your parents' lonely graves
think of everything forgotten
and ashamed
throughout the centuries
the dog on the side of the road
the wheelchaired whore
on Larkin Street
imagine every ignoble
and embarrassing death
since the beginning of time

and you'll begin to understand
that her scorn
is just the gray dust drifting about the surface
of some planet that will never
be named
and the last look on her face
just the silence that comes
at 3 a.m. after the sounds
of trains far off
in the night
have gone quiet.

AS EDITH PIAF SINGS HER BROKEN HEART

Early afternoon in the Tenderloin.

The sun glints on wheelchairs and crutches
and broken glass.

I'm hiding from the world
in this little café

and there's a man
sprawled on the sidewalk
next to a walker made of tin.

No one bothers
to check if he is ill or dead,

all of us
as indifferent as the sun.

Another man scours the ground
for things to smoke or to eat

as Edith Piaf sings
her broken heart

and I sit here with a beer and money in my pocket
not knowing whether to feel lucky
or ashamed.

THE TROUBLE WITH MOST POETRY

is that it's just a mess of stillborn
words serving only to poison

the beauty
it claims to serve,

like bricks around a garden
making a tomb.

THE DARK LIKE A FINELY CUT COAT

I walk the city
filled with a music
born of lonely ghosts too much in love
with the sorrow of the world
to ever let it go
it leads me through silent alleys
and unnamed streets
through graveyards of days abandoned
before they were born
I follow it to the tops of hills
that look out over the city
into yellowlit windows
of old apartment buildings
framing shadows of lonely women
too beautiful to ever speak my name
I follow it to North Beach cafès
sprawled out beneath Van Gogh stars
let me have another drink, beautiful waitress
let me be the sweat on the necks of the sad dancers
in the nudie bars strung out along Broadway
let me wear the dark like a finely cut coat
and parade it through the streets
among the saints and the drunks
let the emptiness of it all transmogrify into this music
that has found me
let me take the great fear of the world
inside me like a drug
and free you of it
for the rest of your days
let the music take me to these ragged cliffs
high above the ocean at the edge of the world
I'll throw myself into the terrible
beautiful grayblue sea
and you'll never see
my face again.

LIKE MARKET ST. NEON

Let's wander the streets
of the City and lose ourselves
in the grand and beautiful decay
as suicides fall like wounded
angels from the Golden Gate
and drunken lovers kiss
in the evening's mist
let's marvel at the pretty girls
and boys on every corner
their faces built to break
every heart
as the junkies nod in
Tenderloin rooms
and the sad ghosts of poets
roam the night planting
blue flowers in the cracks
of North Beach sidewalks
we'll visit the soft smoky rooms
of Chinatown
as sad women sway
to jukebox songs
with hipster kids in Mission bars
drunk on cheap beer and irony
as the skinny hooker by the firehouse
asks me what it is I'm looking for
and I have no answer
other than my desire
for you to stay just a little
while more
and hold my hand as we watch
the love and despair shining
like Market St. neon
through the early morning rain
as the sirens play for us
such crazy songs.

MURIO'S TROPHY ROOM

It wasn't so long ago
that this Haight Street bar
was a dark and rundown
punk rock dive,
beautiful in its way,
with a jukebox as good as
any in town;

a perfect haven from the San Francisco
afternoon, from the mean-faced runaways
and sad-eyed addicts
dealing and begging on
the crowded lonely sidewalks.

But at some point I guess
they raised the rent
or the owner lost the lease
and for months the place
was boarded up
like a ramshackle tomb.

I went by last week
and it was open again,
transformed into a generic, brightly lit
hotspot for tourists,
big ugly windows
letting in the all the terrible
light of the day,

all the old magic gone,
not even the jukebox was spared.

Sweetheart,
we live in a world
without mercy, conscience
or style;

it tears down our love
and kicks our hearts
out into these awful streets,

dismantles our lives
like shut down buildings.
replacing every beautiful thing
with a sadness
too deep and wide
to cross.

THE FAILURE OF LOVE AND EVERYTHING

We are the wasted armies of the ages,
we are every ticket that didn't win,
the view from every window of every shitty hotel
in every shitty town you can imagine.
We are the need for one more drink
just after 2 a.m.
as the heartless bartender says
it's too late, too late,
go home.
We're the wreck on the freeway
the people drive past
and forget,
we're the poster children
for the failure of love
and everything.
Yet even now,
after everything,
on nights like this
I can still get drunk enough
to miss you
something awful.

TO MY ASTROLOGIST FRIEND

You'll probably say it's just my
Scorpio ascending in the third house
of something or other,

but I don't think the stars
have much to say

about our lives
and what we've made of them,

far away as they are, and consumed
with their own burning.

But if you want to chart the course
of your sad little boat
by the light of their lonely ghosts,

dreaming it will guide you to some
imagined shore,

it's your own business;

I suspect they will not know or care,
caught and falling
in the same night as you.

TARA SINGS
for Tara DeMoulin

We're outside that famous café in North Beach
a sunny afternoon in July
we're at our sidewalk tables with wine
and cappuccino
me and the other sad old poets
suntanned tourists
and the neighborhood folk
a man sits on the sidewalk
with a guitar
singing a Simon and Garfunkel song
Bridge Over Troubled Water
and it's not bad but nobody's
paying much attention
and then Tara walks by
like something from a movie
like something left over from better times
with her legs and her hair and her smile and her everything
she's got a bag of apples from the local market
she stops and sets it down
and sings along with the man
on the sidewalk
she's got a voice
that knows what music is
and she sings like nobody's watching
but everybody's watching
the sad old poets smile and nod
the tourists take pictures
and the man on the sidewalk plays
like he truly has a reason to
for the first time in his life
and Tara nails it
she brings it home
and when it's over she smiles
grabs her bag
and continues on her way
the man with the guitar
looks around and says

that there was Tara
now that she's gone
I can only sing the blues
and he does
but nobody much cares
because Tara's
blocks away now
the magic of the day
trailing after her like pixie dust
the tourists still snapping
pictures like madmen
trying so hard for a piece
of her soul.

FUCK THE DEAD

I woke up and forgot how to write a poem
and decided that writing poems was stupid.

I couldn't think of anything to love
and decided love was stupid, too.

I went outside and the streets clanged with loneliness,
the people dulled and drunk with suffering;
some blatantly so, others
going through the motions of hiding it.

I decided that suffering was stupid because it was useless,
more useless even than poetry,

and I suddenly felt outside it all, bigger than
the living and their hand-me-down sufferings,
better than the smugness of the dead.

Fuck the dead and the living alike, I thought, what
good are they to me?

I wandered through it all like some stillborn ghost,
a thing unto myself, inscrutable and alien.

But within an hour I was tired of that
so I fell in love with the next useless thing I saw
and wrote a stupid poem about it.

SOME THINGS

There's not much
that ever comes
to anything

and you understand this
more than me.

I accept it in the abstract
but not so much in the heart
or the gut or wherever it is
that really matters.

The music dies out
the stage is pulled down
the circus moves along.

There's just this space now
where some things
used to be.

I guess there's not much else
to say about it

and I'm the only one
who'll bother
to remember.

THE GHOST OF US

The ghost of us visits me at night, of course;
a sad pretty music that sings with the dark.
But it doesn't leave with the coming dawn,
doesn't burn off with the morning fog.

The ghost of us has no fear of the sun.

This afternoon it gazed back at me from the dirty mirror
behind the counter of a Tenderloin cafè.
It clung to me like a lover through the streets of Chinatown.
The ghost of us sits with me now
at my favorite table at a North Beach bar.
It remembers the pretty waitress and Crazy Henry
sitting on his stool, gleefully cursing passersby.

The ghost of us waves to the friendly bartender
at the gay karaoke joint.

The ghost of us is not a malicious shade,
like most of us it's a slave to its nature
and means no real harm.

Sure, it makes me drink whiskey and cry at 4 a.m.
but it keeps me company and tells me stories
when I would otherwise be alone.

Some days I hide from it,
some days I call it dirty names and threaten
to banish it to hell, but I don't think I'll ever
really send it away for good.

The ghost of us tried to visit you
once or twice
but tells me you were preoccupied
with living things.

The ghost of us is as lonely as anyone

and just as frightened of being forgotten.

It lives behind my eyes,
giving them that look my friends
will, on occasion, describe
as haunted.

THE WORLD FOR BEING WHAT IT IS

The day crashes
down upon me
like a wounded thing
from the sky,
and recognizing
it cannot be saved
is a freedom of sorts.
I'm hungover on a
Sunday morning
and the ageless sorrow of everything
has found me again.
I surrender to it
in Chinatown alleyways
and North Beach bars,
drinking beer and forgiving myself
for all the good things left
undone,
all the good love left
to wither,
forgiving the world
for being what it is,
asking a similar mercy
in return.
The jazz in this place
is bad
but the blond rich woman
in the flowered dress
drinking martinis
is amazing.
She sees I'm looking at her breasts
and smiles across
the rubble of the afternoon.

SOMEONE IN MY BUILDING

Indian summer, San Francisco;
it's 4 a.m. and my window is open
to the warm breeze and early morning darkness.

An ambulance roars by on its way to some misfortune
and someone in my building is screaming that she wants to die.

And that's just the way of things; you're busy trying to breathe
or love or enjoy your tea

and out there in the dark there's always someone wanting to die
or someone dying who would rather be otherwise engaged,

uniformed people walking poker-faced
through doorways into the ruins of peoples' lives

and all you can do is accept it and get on with things,

forgetting as best you can that you're just another
tattered thing waiting for your turn at sorrow.

The woman in my building is still screaming her pain
but the night is otherwise pleasant.
I'm no longer sleepy and pour a glass of wine and sit by
the window awhile,

taking in the warm summer air and the terror of things.

HOW WE LIVE

I think in general it's most honest
to acknowledge
that things are here for a time
and then are gone

and there's not much else
to say about it.

It's not a particularly
romantic notion

or good talk at parties,
I know,

yet there it is.

But see, the potential for beauty lies
not in this truth

but in how we live with it.

LOVE AND HOPE

Honey we had such a good thing going
back before we ruined it
with talk of promises
and dreams

and all that other pretty junk
that only served to break
our silly hearts

love and hope never brought us
nothing but pain

honey can we start again
I miss the way you laugh

this time we'll not speak
of forever

let's just fuck
and watch TV.

MEAT

For a good portion of my life I couldn't figure out why people
liked steak.

I had nothing against meat, I liked meat just fine-
but in my parents' house, in the summer months,
every Sunday evening we had steak for dinner.

We were to consider it a treat, a delicacy,
something to look forward to.

When I saw people eating steaks on television or in movies
it seemed like a good thing, and their eyes lit up
when they spoke of it.

But when my father put the plate in front of me
the slab of meat was always gray and joyless.
It tasted like nothing and each leathery piece was a chore to chew.

Our steaks were like that because that's
how my mom imagined they were supposed to be.

My dad would bring in the platter from the backyard grill
and present it to my mother for inspection.

They're not done, my mom would invariably say, *look at all that blood!*
It's not blood, my dad would reply, *it's juice.*
We can't eat them like that, take them back and cook them
until they're done!

My dad would say something under his breath and then take
the meat away and bring it back a while later
when there was no more juice or blood.

Then we'd all sit there at the table not saying much of anything.
We'd smother the meat in A1 Sauce and chew and chew and chew.

I'd put ketchup on mine, place it between two pieces

of wonder bread and pretend it was a hamburger.

My mother would scold me, telling me I didn't know
how to appreciate good things.

At some point at a friend's house, a restaurant, somewhere,
I had a steak in the manner they were meant to be consumed:
it was seared on the outside, but the thick cube of meat
was tender and juicy and red just beneath the surface.

I was startled at first; it was like nothing I'd ever experienced.
It tasted like all the colors of life and death and the blood and juice
dribbled down my chin and onto the plate, and I sopped it up
with a piece of bread and when it was gone I wanted more.

Things in general suddenly made a bit more sense to me,
and I wondered what else I had been missing out on.

MISSION STREET, DECEMBER

The soft yellow dream of street lamps
brings a sadness that pushes
the heart,

strange clouds gather and the air
smells of coming rain.

I wander Mission Street sidewalks
not wanting to be anywhere,

still haunted by the pretty dream
of being something more than death,

even now determined
to salvage some scraps of joy
from the wreckage of things,

maintaining a belief
in common miracles.

Bits of kindness scatter
like sidewalk leaves
not yet trampled,

and remnants of abandoned
beauty line the streets
in gilded flakes.

I collect them in my pockets
to carry home,

walking quickly now
as soon the rain
will come

down upon it all
like some god thing's
useless tears.

MOST OF WHAT THEY'VE SAID

Friends, there's not much
to it, after all.

Years pass, things fall away.

Most of what they've said isn't true.

There are precious few things
that need remembering:

keep bitterness at bay
as best you can,

kindness whenever possible.

Listen to the ancient music
of things

and let it guide you.

Seek out the deeper joy
within the blanketing sorrow.

Embrace it and become
whatever it is you are.

CEREMONY

Tonight I got drunk
and whispered your name
like an incantation in the dark.

I lit a roomful of candles
to the memory of the smell
of your hair and the taste
of your skin,

the music of your laughter
and the last time I saw your face,

as false and as beautiful
as any god that was
ever dreamed.

THE MUSIC OF THINGS

It's midnight
in downtown San Francisco.

I'm alone in my apartment
with wine and old records,

while outside the city

reels with desperate joy,
gaudy tragedy

and a never-ending hunger
for what, it doesn't know;

hipsters, losers
drunks and whores,

all sprawling on the streets
in an ancient, lonely dance,

the joy and the sorrow
of everything,
the beauty and the terror,
merged into a single
terrible song.

I breathe it in
and sing it out of tune
with the people of the night
and the dead man on my record

until the woman upstairs
comes down
and tells me to keep it quiet.

I can tell by her eyes
she means business

and has no interest
in the music of things.

I feel a bit sorry for her
as I listen to her stomping
angrily back up the stairs.

I pour another wine,
choose another record
and settle in
for the long night ahead.

THE NORTH BEACH POETS

The North Beach poets meet
each Wednesday night at the bar.

They sit at their table in the middle of the place,
they drink and talk loudly
in the dim light.

They shout and pound their
fists upon the wood.
They talk of ANARCHY
and COMMUNISM
and other things that failed.

They talk as if it mattered,
and if you've had a few drinks
you'll almost believe them.

Sometimes they read their poems
in loud and authoritative voices
and their poems are filled with words
like LIBERTY, FREEDOM
and OPPRESSION.

They decry the evils of WAR
as if no one had ever thought
to consider such things.

They read their poems with great passion,
they read their poems as if they believed them,

as if those responsible
for things like WAR
POVERTY
and OPPRESSION

would cease their shenanigans
if they would only pause a moment

and listen to the North Beach poets.

Maybe this is so, but I
have my doubts

and the North Beach poets drink
and shout and pound their table deep
into the night.

Me, I just wish they'd quiet down a bit.

I've got my own
poems to wrangle with
and right now I'm trying to figure out
how to spell the way she laughed
and remember how the night felt as it
came apart in my hands.

LIKE NOBODY EVER TOLD YOU

You wear your damage
like a fresh haircut
or a favorite dress
on Sunday afternoons
as you drift about the city
with the other ghosts
you carry it like a bag of free samples
handing it out to everyone you see
like it was the one thing in life they were missing
like nobody ever told you
your damage
is yesterday's news that nobody
read the first time around
unless you know how to make it pretty
unless you know how to make it dance
like the girls
at the Condor Club
the ones you spend your rent money on
for the chance to taste their sweat
if you don't know how to work
your damage like that
if you don't know how to make it sing
like a beast on fire
you may as well keep it to yourself
because nobody wants to know
even if they tell you otherwise
and smile awkwardly
when you offer it like a gift
they'll thank you softly
and when they turn the corner
they'll drop it in the outstretched hands
of a dirty man on the sidewalk
like a half eaten sandwich
they didn't order
anyway.

REPORT

It's after midnight and I'm standing on a concrete platform
waiting on a train,

gazing across an empty parking lot at the lights of cars
as they move along the freeway.

I'm missing you like a limb, or something
I once believed in.

I wish the world wouldn't always boil down
to such things but it somehow always does.

The train arrives and I shove myself on,
pressed between the eyes of strangers,
drunk and unknowing.

I study the graceless faces,
noting each one you'd imagine
more beautiful than mine.

ROCKTOP PROPHETS

for H.K. Rainey

The fog hangs about the Carmel shore
like something more or less poetic,
harboring lonely secrets and treasures
stolen by the sea.
Once alone upon the landscape,
the dead poet's house is now caught
between the homes of the rich and boring
people he despised.
We search for his ghost but it has fled
deep into the granite and cypress,
just as he foretold.
So we walk along the beach,
filling our pockets with pretty debris.
We sit upon the sand and laugh at empty things,
while prophets sit like drunken
Buddhas atop the rocks, their wisdom
less than the chatter of gulls.
Our laughter drifts with ghosts
into the fog and this is magic enough.
Since the dawn of time hearts
have broken for so much less.

SAD LITTLE MONSTERS

Writing poems you'll never read
is the only way I can speak to you anymore.

There was a time
when those who mete out slivers of grace
upon the world like occasional rain

spoke our names with a certain fondness

but at some point mercy had other things to do

and they rounded up all the soft things
and spirited them to someplace cold

and burned every map that could ever take us back
to all the pretty things we said.

These days the sad little monsters we sometimes
call our hearts
keep us from sleep with their lonely stirrings
and strange desires,

though we drown them like kittens
again and again.

The stars will fall and the moon
will break its promises

but honey, let's not squander our sorrow
all in one place;

it's early yet and the night
has more to say.

IN HONOR OF THE NEW YEAR

January again,
and outside it's just
the same sad ghosts,
the same tenuous dreams
drifting about the crumpled streets,
caught and torn
on ringwire fences
and the branches of trees,
forgotten on sidewalks
with the garbage and umbrellas,
the endless gray of the pavement and the sky
as pretty and as terrifying
as it was yesterday.
In honor of the new year,
I feel I should have something more
to say about it all,
but I don't.
I turn from it
and you are there
with a bottle of something.
We pour two glasses,
we drink and laugh,
our bodies find each other
and celebrate the fact of that
and nothing else in particular.
There is renewal enough in this.
We lie together
beneath the window,
listening
to the sirens
and the lonely
sing.

SWAYING

You once imagined me beautiful
but in truth I was as common as a wasted day
and you were just another story
nobody wanted to hear.
There is a kind of beauty
like a wound we don't
recover from,
the kind most will never see,
blind as old gods banished
and forgotten into darkness.
Our addled hearts lead us
down dubious avenues
and each choice we make
murders infinite possibilities;
see us standing on street corners
with our aborted lives still
inside us like mangled dreams
we refuse to abandon.
I stand at the window
swaying to the shattered
music of the day,
looking out upon this
terrible city,
my heart full of dust
and that time I made you laugh.

BLOWING UP

He gave my poems back to me and said,
these are okay, man, but there's a bitterness in them.
Bitterness won't get you anywhere in life.

Okay, I said, thanks.

It's simple, he said, you get out of life what you put into it,
everybody gets exactly what they deserve, see?

I didn't find that notion particularly
plausible or comforting, but I let him go on.

Life's a game, he said, you either get rich
or you eat shit and die, it's as simple as that.

I'd never thought of it in exactly that way,
but I figured he must know something
because he was 29 years old,
edited a magazine
and had a pretty wife and a big house
in Mexico.

I came from nothing, he said,
I used to starve in little rooms for years,
living on tap water and stale bread.
But I worked, man, I worked 'round the clock
and look at me now, I'm gonna blow up real soon.

I wasn't quite sure if blowing up meant
becoming really famous or going on a killing spree
but I'm assuming he meant the former.

When I blow up, he continued,
I'm not gonna be greedy about it.
I just wanna inspire people
and piss off my haters,

use their energy to fuel my greatness.
I'll be free while they work their shitty
20 dollar an hour jobs for the rest of their lives.

I wanted to ask him about those 20 dollar an hour jobs
and how I might get one, but he went on:

Anyway, he said, poetry isn't the way to go.
It doesn't pay and the only way you'll get famous
is if you rap it, you know, hip hop style.

Well, I thought, shit.

Me, he said, I get paid 40 cents a word for writing bullshit.
Memoirs, restaurant reviews, anything but poetry, man.
You just need to learn how things work!

But don't worry, man, you can make it, too.
You just gotta work hard, every day.
You gotta write 2000 words every day!

It was 4 o' clock on a Sunday afternoon
and all I'd accomplished thus far
was drink four cups of coffee,
fuck around on Facebook and take a bath.

Real writers, he said, they figure out
the way things work and write all day
and all night until they blow up!

I thought about the writers I knew
and I don't think many of them understood
much about the way things worked.

Most of them spent as much time
in bars and jails and nuthouses
as they did writing,

but I guess they weren't the real writers
he was talking about.
They didn't get paid 40 cents a word
and I guess most of them would eventually
just end up eating shit and dying.

But they were beautiful in their way-
they had strange light in their eyes
and sometimes said wise and funny things
that helped me through the lonely hours.

Anyway, he said, I've wasted enough time with you.
I'm gonna go get some real writing done
and if you're smart you'll do the same.

So I had a beer and another bath
and pondered things a bit.

Thinking about how it all worked
just made me tired, so I took a nap
and when I got up I wrote another poem.

TAKE THEM

The tiny moments of light
that sometime come
in between everything else

are what we wait for,

are what make all the
sad and empty hours
worthwhile.

Such moments come
only of their own accord

and are often few
and far between.

Sometimes
it seems the waiting
is all there is.

It may seem
like a rotten deal,
and maybe so,

but when they finally come
they are so beautiful,
so perfect.

They are a magic
that trumps even death.

So be patient.

Wait for them
and when they arrive

recognize them

and be grateful.

Take them
and run.

THE NEXT THING

At this point I can't begin
to guess what's
left of me.

Sometimes you lose the rhythm of things,
the music goes funny
and the sky forgets your name.

I just know the demons
aren't going anywhere soon,
so I drink with them on Sunday afternoons,
trying to negotiate some kind of
workable deal,

while down in the alley
a withered woman begs quarters
from confused tourists.

She's having a bad time of it

as the girls stand outside the nudie bars,
half naked and smoking,
as beautiful and as mean
as the sun.

I watch them as the pretty waitress
brings my medicine

and think about how I'll
have to go back to work tomorrow,
hungover
and with little sleep,

and how the waitress
and the girls outside the clubs
one day won't be pretty,
or even alive,

and I'm feeling kind of sad for everything
and how there's nothing to be done
for any of it,

as we all go about our business,
waiting for the next thing
to break.

THE OLD LADY ON POST STREET

She's either waiting on a bus
or just simply standing there.

I guess it doesn't matter much
either way.

TRADE

I would trade
all of my poems

for one moment
of your drunken
laughter.

I'm
serious.

THE SONG OF WHATEVER'S LEFT OF US

Baby, let's get up,
get dressed, and sing the song
of whatever's left of us.

Everything's older and sadder
than we could have ever dreamed,

but a strange music
still plays at the heart
of the silence of things.

Prayers rise up
like the honking of horns
above endless miles
of traffic that will never
move,

as we make our way
through Chinatown
on a Sunday afternoon.

The ducks and the chickens and the geese
stuffed in the cages in the trucks
outside the butcher shops

try and tell us things,

but we hurry past
to our favorite table
up above Broadway
and Columbus

where we drink with the emptiness
and the monsters we've become
until everything is laughter again.

We bargain with the dark,

and buy a map
that leads us to an unmarked grave
at the edge of town

where we dig up the abandoned beauty of forgotten things.

We take it inside us
and burn

like we'd never
forgotten how.

THE THINGS THE PRETTY GIRLS SAY

It's the last day of Summer
as I sit at a sidewalk table
at a North Beach café
clinging to the hours
like a drowning man,
and after a few glasses of wine
I believe all the stories
the sun has to tell,
I believe the things the pretty girls say
with their dream-fed smiles
and the movement of their tanned
and skinny arms,
and all these people at their tables
just like mine,
with their wine and their
tiny plates of food, their porcelain wives
and glimmering children,
surely they understand, just as I do,
that the world is made of magic after all,
and light will have the final say,
and the dark is just a nasty story
told by some demented dwarf
in a lonely basement
to keep the children in line,
and death is just a baseless rumor,
obsolete and powerless
in the face of one last hour
of sunlight,
another glass of wine,
and the smell of this woman
at the table
next to mine.

TIME AND SPACE

If you are not at least trying
to do or be
something beautiful

I do not understand
the point of you.

Your existence is an obstacle,
something in the way.

And let's not argue
about the nature
of beauty or its
definitions;

you know it
when it is there
and when it
is not.

If you can't see the path
you can feel your way
through the dark
with the rest of us.

If you are not at least trying
to do or be
something beautiful

you are wasting
time and space
and we don't have
enough of either.

UNION SQUARE IN THE RAIN

It's Tuesday afternoon and it's been raining
three days straight
the gray sky is heavy with great
gray clouds and beneath it
gray faced people with gray scarves
gray coats and gray umbrellas
drift about the gray sidewalks
of Union Square
while gray cars and buses
amble toward some
destination of gray.

I marvel at all the subtle
shades, some dark
some light, some deep
and blue
all of it swirling about me
and the air smells of
sad soft memories as
I dream of all the ghosts
I've ever known.

I'm standing on a corner
beside a gray haired woman
our eyes meet and she says
what an ugly day and I politely
disagree.

WEAR YOUR SORROW

We wake to the day at hand
like another thing we never wanted
but can't quite bring ourselves
to give away.

Outside, the billboards
and the faces advertise
the latest version of fear

but we've already bought
the deluxe edition
with the lifetime warranty,

so we find a place
where we can rest a bit
and get some poison in our guts
to keep us safe awhile
from the things that chase us.

The world's no different
from anyone,
just another sad thing
trying to make it through.

On nights without sleep
it cries for lost things
and the lack of what it once
dreamed to be.

Wear your sorrow like a favorite dress
and I'll sing you songs of no second chances;

our only crime is imagining the world
more beautiful than it was born to be.

If we met it on the street today

it wouldn't even know our names

but I swear to you it loved us once
and you can't buy that kind of thing anymore,
not even on computers.

THE DYING LIGHT LIKE A FAVORITE MOVIE

Joy even now

despite the eventual doom
of yourself
and everything you've ever loved

joy even now

even if it's frowned upon
by old women in purple pantsuits

and old men with eyes
like stars that died

see, death is just a coward
death is just as frightened
as the rest of us

otherwise it wouldn't be so mean

joy even now

because you've got nothing better to do

because sorrow's not going anywhere

it's patient
it will wait until you're done

joy even now

despite the crumbling infrastructure
of your city
and the crumbling infrastructure
of yourself

even if the cool kids wear it

on ironic t-shirts

even if the cool kids tell you
it was so six months ago

even if there's no future in it

joy even now

even as they tell you
your time is done

even as they tell you it's not
about you anymore

even if they didn't
mention you in the credits

and all your best bits
were edited out
due to time constraints

and your name is spelled wrong
in the book of life

even if they're lining up
to pull you off the stage

and talk shit about the relevance
of you and your scene

joy even now

because the unjoyful are never pretty
and are never any fun
to drink with

joy even now
even if you have no permit
even if you have no right

even if you can't save everyone
even if you can't save anyone

because people are gonna tell you
your life is wrong
and your poems are wrong

no matter what you do

they're gonna tell you that your sex
and your race
and your gender are obsolete

but don't worry about it
we can watch the dying light
like a favorite movie
we already know the ending to

and the winners will win
but us losers we know how to dance

and I don't even care what time it is

the last bus home
left
hours ago.

WELL ENOUGH

I will give you this:

I am lazy and mostly
without purpose,

but in my favor I wish harm
on no one.

I strive for days of scattered wonder,
a few hours now and then
to marvel at the sun
and the rain
and the ongoing
music of things.

I want wine and laughter,
days in quiet rooms.

I want time and space enough
to write this poem,

I don't care if I've written it before.

All the rest I'll sort out
as best I can,

muddling through the days
as long as I'm allowed,

every now and then

living well enough
to make the dying worthwhile.

SUNDAY AT VESUVIO

With a bit more effort
we could be beautiful,
famous and rich

but the sun
and the wine
make me lazy.

We sit at our favorite table
and the breeze that drifts
through the open window
distracts me from dreams of commerce.

A man plays soft jazz in the alley below

while confused tourists
dutifully photograph
whatever they're told

as the homeless and the hustlers
the sad drunk poets and the pretty girls
in pretty dresses
drift along Broadway
beneath the North Beach sun.

There's a pure and strange
magic to it
and I cannot look away.

I don't know if life
was meant
to be any more than this
and I don't much care.

I set aside what it is
I'm working on

and breathe it all in
and out

and in
again.

ACKNOWLEDGMENTS

Some of the poems in this collection have appeared in the following publications— *Alternative Reel*, *Bicycle Review*, *Bold Monkey*, *Catamaran Literary Review*, *Chiron Review*, *Crisis Chronicles*, *Dead Snakes*, *Fried Chicken and Coffee*, *Gin Mill Cowboy*, *Gutter Eloquence*, *Least Bittern Press*, *Litup Magazine*, *Mas Tequila Review*, *Out of Our*, *Poetic Pinup*, *Red Fez*, *Regardless of Authority*, *Remark*, *Rusty Truck*, *This is Poetry*, *Up The Staircase Quarterly*, *Words Dance*, *Zygote in My Coffee*.

ABOUT THE AUTHOR

William Taylor Jr. lives and writes in the Tenderloin neighborhood of San Francisco. His work has been published widely in journals across the globe, including *The New York Quarterly*, *The Chiron Review*, and *Catamaran Literary Reader*. He is the author of numerous books of poetry and *An Age of Monsters*, a collection of short fiction. He is a Pushcart Prize nominee and was a recipient of the 2013 Kathy Acker Award.

WORDS DANCE PUBLISHING has one aim:

To spread mind-blowing / heart-opening poetry.

Words Dance artfully & carefully wrangles words that were born to dance wildly in the heart-mind matrix. Rich, edgy, raw, emotionally-charged energy balled up & waiting to whip your eyes wild; we rally together words that were written to make your heart go boom right before they slay your mind.

Words Dance Publishing is an independent press out of Pennsylvania. We work closely & collaboratively with all of our writers to ensure that their words continue to breathe in a sound & stunning home. Most importantly though, we leave the windows in these homes unlocked so you, the reader, can crawl in & throw one fuck of a house party.

To learn more about our books, authors, events & Words Dance Poetry Magazine, visit:

WORDSDANCE.COM

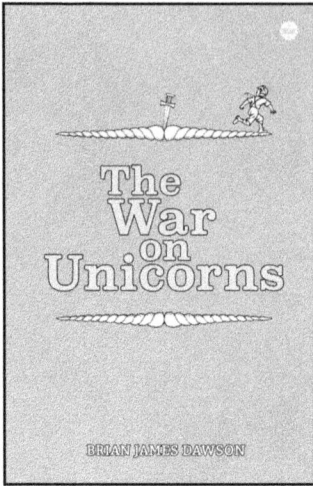

Other titles available from
WORDS DANCE PUBLISHING

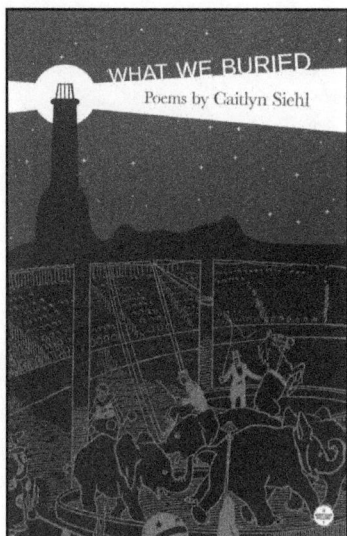

WHAT WE BURIED
Poetry by Caitlyn Siehl

| $12 | 64 pages | 5.5" x 8.5" | softcover |

ISBN: 978-0615985862

GOODREADS CHOICE AWARD NOMINEE FOR POETRY (2014)

This book is a cemetery of truths buried alive. The light draws you in where you will find Caitlyn there digging. When you get close enough, she'll lean in & whisper, Baby, buried things will surface no matter what, get to them before they get to you first. Her unbounded love will propel you to pick up a shovel & help— even though the only thing you want to do is kiss her lips, kiss her hands, kiss every one of her stretch marks & the fire that is raging in pit of her stomach. She'll see your eyes made of devour & sadness, she'll hug you & say, Baby, if you eat me alive, I will cut my way out of your stomach. Don't let this be your funeral. Teach yourself to navigate the wound.

"It takes a true poet to write of love and desire in a way that manages to surprise and excite. Caitlyn Siehl does this in poem after poem and makes it seem effortless. Her work shines with a richness of language and basks in images that continue to delight and astound with multiple readings. *What We Buried* is a treasure from cover to cover."

— **WILLIAM TAYLOR JR.**
Author of *An Age of Monsters*

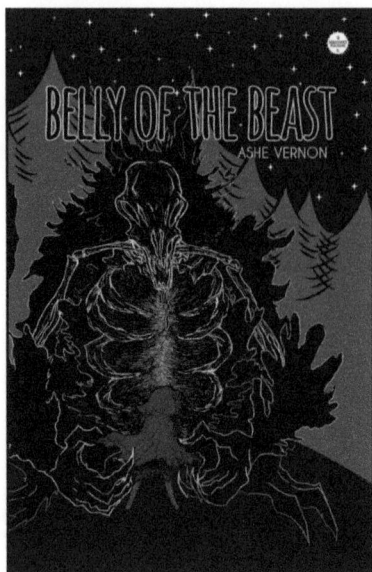

BELLY OF THE BEAST
Poetry by Ashe Vernon

| $12 | 82 pages | 5.5" x 8.5" | softcover |

ISBN: 978-0692300541

"Into the *Belly of the Beast* we crawl with Ashe as our guide; into the dark visceral spaces where love, lust, descent and desire work their transformative magic and we find ourselves utterly altered in the reading. A truly gifted poet and truth-spiller, Ashe's metaphors create images within images, leading us to question the subjective truths, both shared and hidden, in personal relationship – to the other, and to oneself. Unflinching in her approach, her poetry gives voice to that which most struggle to admit – even if only to themselves. And as such, *Belly of the Beast* is a work of startling courage and rich depth – a darkly delicious pleasure."

— AMY PALKO
Goddess Guide, Digital Priestess & Writer

"It isn't often you find a book of poetry that is as unapologetic, as violent, as moving as this one. Ashe's writing is intense and visceral. You feel the punch in your gut while you're reading, but you don't question it. You know why it's there and you almost welcome it."

— CAITLYN SIEHL
Author of *What We Buried*

"The poems you are about to encounter are the fierce time capsules of girl-hood, girded with sharp elbows, surprise kisses, the meanders of wander-lust. We need voices this strong, this true for the singing reminds us that we are not alone, that someone, somewhere is listening for the faint pulse that is our wish to be seen. Grab hold, this voice will be with us forever."

— RA WASHINGTON
GuidetoKulchurCleveland.com

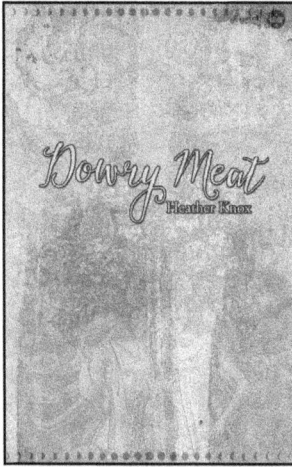

DOWRY MEAT

Poetry by Heather Knox

| $12 | 110 pages | 5.5" x 8.5" | softcover |

ISBN: 978-0692398494

Heather Knox's *Dowry Meat* is a gorgeous, tough-as-nails debut that arrives on your doorstep hungry and full of dark news. There's damage here, and obsession, and more haunted beauty in the wreckage of just about everything—relationships, apartment clutter, rough sex, the body, and of course the just-post apocalypse—than you or I could hope to find on our own. These are poems that remind us not that life is hard—that's old news—but that down there in the gravel and broken glass is where the truth-worth-hearing lies, and maybe the life worth living. If you were a city, Knox tells us, unflinching as always, *I'd... read your graffiti. Drink your tap water./Feel your smog and dirt stick to my sweat... If you were a city, I'd expect to be robbed.*

— **JON LOOMIS**

Author of *Vanitas Motel (winner of the FIELD prize)* and *The Pleasure Principle*

"Heather Knox's debut collection is a lyric wreath made of purulent ribbon and the most inviting of thorns. Tansy and tokophobia, lachrymosity and lavage are braided together in this double collection, which marries a sci-fi Western narrative to a lyric sequence. Both elapse in an impossible location made of opposites—futuristic nostalgia, or erotic displeasure—otherwise known as the universe in which we (attempt to) live."

— **JOYELLE MCSWEENEY**

Author of *The Necropastoral: Poetry, Media, Occults & Salamandrine: 8 Gothics*

"*Dowry Meat*'s apocalyptic fever dream myth-making bleeds into what we might call the poetry of witness or the tradition of the confessional, except that these lines throb with lived experience and a body isn't necessarily a confession. Heather Knox's poems are beautifully wrought and beautifully raw."

— **DORA MALECH**

Author of *Shore Ordered Ocean & Say So*

Other titles available from
WORDS DANCE PUBLISHING

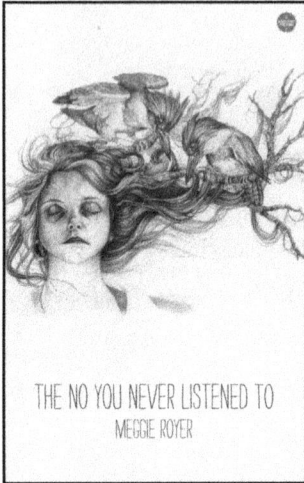

THE NO YOU NEVER LISTENED TO
Poetry by Meggie Royer

| $14 | 142 pages | 5.5" x 8.5" | softcover |

ISBN: 978-0692463635

THE NO YOU NEVER LISTENED TO
MEGGIE ROYER

"It's a strange thing when the highest praise you can offer for someone's work is, "I wish this didn't exist," but that was the refrain that echoed in my head after I read Meggie Royer's third book.

As fans of her work know, Meggie takes the universal and makes it personal. With *The No You Never Listened To*, she takes the personal and makes it universal. As a sexual assault survivor, Meggie is well-acquainted with trauma: the aftermath, the guilt, the anger. She has never shied away from taking Hemingway's advice – write hard and clear about what hurts – and that strength has never been more of an asset than with this body of work.

The No You Never Listened To is the book you will wish you'd had when trauma climbed into your bed. It is the book you will give to friends who are dragged from their "before" into a dark and terrifying "after". And yes, it is the book you will wish didn't exist.

But it is also the one that will remind you, in your darkest moments, where the blame really belongs. It will remind you that your memory will not always be an enemy. And it will remind you that none of us have ever been alone in this."

— CLAIRE BIGGS
To Write Love on Her Arms Editor / Writer

"Nietzsche once warned us to be careful gazing into the abyss, that we run the risk of staring so long that the void consumes us. The poems in this book were born of the abyss, of conflict & trauma & survival. And through these poems, Meggie Royer stares – hard, unflinching, courageous – and instead of gazing back, the abyss looks away."

— WILLIAM JAMES
Drunk In A Midnight Choir editor & author of *rebel hearts & restless ghosts*

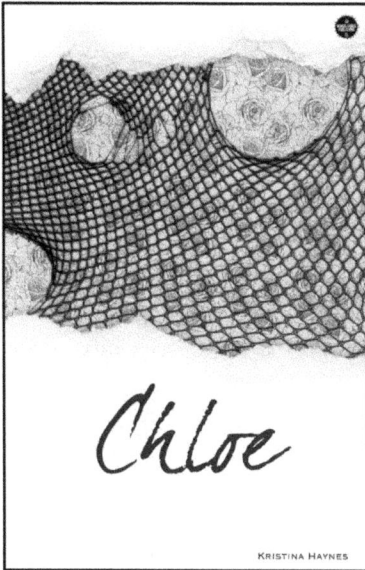

CHLOE
Poetry by Kristina Haynes

| $12 | 110 pages | 5.5" x 8.5" | softcover |

ISBN: 978-0692386637

Chloe is brave and raw, adolescence mixed with salt. These poems are about how hungry we've been, how foolish, how lonely. Chloe is not quite girl nor woman, full of awkward bravery. Kristina is an electric voice that pulls Chloe apart page after page, her heartbreaks, her too many drinks, her romantic experiences of pleasure and pain. Chloe and Kristina make a perfect team to form an anthem for girls everywhere, an anthem that reassures us we deserve to take up space. Indeed, when I met Chloe, I too thought "This is the closest I've been to anybody in months."

— **MEGGIE ROYER**
Author of *Survival Songs*
and *Healing Old Wounds with New Stitches*

"*Chloe* is one of the most intimate books you'll read all year. Chloe is my new best friend. I want to eat burnt popcorn on her couch and watch Friends reruns. I want to borrow her clothing, write on her walls in lipstick. Chloe is not your dream girl. She doesn't have everything figured out. She's messy. She's always late. She promises old lovers she'll never call again. She teaches you what the word "indulgence" means. She's wonderful, wonderful, wonderful. In *Chloe*, Kristina Haynes digs into the grittiness of modern womanhood, of mothers and confusion and iPhones and two, maybe three-night-stands. Her truths are caramels on the tongue but are blunter, harsher on the way down. Kristina introduces us to a character I'll be thinking about for a very long time. Go read this book. Then write a poem. Then kiss someone. Then buy an expensive strain of tea and a new pillow. Then go read it again."

— **YASMIN BELKHYR**
Editor-in-Chief at *Winter Tangerine Review*

LITERARY SEXTS
VOLUME 2

A Collection of Short & Sexy Love Poems

| $12 | 76 pages | 5.5" x 8.5" | softcover |

ISBN: 978-0692359594

This is the highly anticipated second volume of Literary Sexts! After over 1,000 copies of Literary Sexts Volume 1 being sold, we are super-excited to bring you a second volume! Literary Sexts is an annual modern day anthology of short love & sexy poems edited by Amanda Oaks & Caitlyn Siehl. These are poems that you would text to your lover. Poems that you would slip into a back pocket, suitcase, wallet or purse on the sly. Poems that you would write on slips of paper & stick under your crush's windshield wiper or pillow. Poems that you would write on a Post-it note & leave on the bathroom mirror. Poems that you would whisper into your lover's ear. Hovering around 40 contributors & 130 poems, this book reads is like one long & very intense conversation between two lovers. It's absolutely breathtaking.

This is for the leather
& the lace of you–

your flushed cheeks
& what set them ablaze.

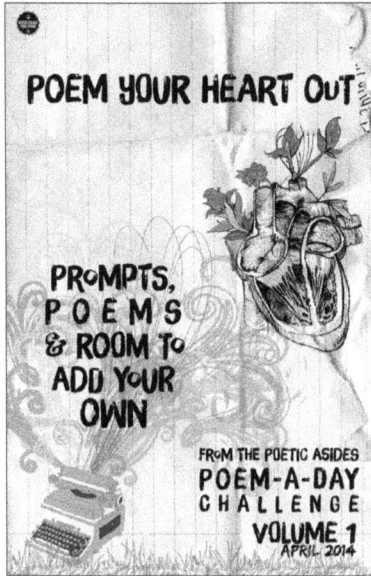

POEM YOUR HEART OUT
Prompts, Poems & Room to Add Your Own
Volume 1

| $15 | 158 pages | 5.5" x 8.5" | softcover |

ISBN: 978-0692317464

PROMPT BOOK • ANTHOLOGY • WORKBOOK

Words Dance Publishing teamed up with the Writer's Digest's Poetic Asides blog to make their Poem-A-Day challenge this year even more spectacular!

Part poetry prompt book, part anthology of the best poems written during the 2014 April PAD (Poem-A-Day) Challenge on the Poetic Asides blog (by way of Writer's Digest) & part workbook, let both, the prompt & poem, inspire you to create your own poetic masterpieces. Maybe you participated in April & want to document your efforts during the month. Maybe you're starting now, like so many before you, with just a prompt, an example poem, & an invitation to poem your heart out! You're encouraged—heck, dared—to write your own poems inside of this book!

This book is sectioned off by Days, each section will hold the prompt for that day, the winning poem for that day & space for you to place the poem you wrote for that day's prompt inside.

Just a few of the guest judges: Amy King, Bob Hicok, Jericho Brown, Nate Pritts, Kristina Marie Darling & Nin Andrews...

Challenge yourself, your friend, a writing workshop or your class to this 30 Day Poem-A-Day Challenge!

THIS IS AN INVITATION TO POEM YOUR HEART OUT!

I EAT CROW + BLUE COLLAR AT BEST
Poetry by Amanda Oaks + Zach Fishel

| $15 | 124 pages | 5.5" x 8.5" | softcover |

Home is where the heart is and both poets' hearts were raised in the Appalachian region of Western Pennsylvania surrounded by coal mines, sawmills, two-bit hotel taverns, farms, churches and cemeteries. These poems take that region by the throat and shake it until it's bloody and then, they breathe it back to life. This book is where you go when you're looking for nostalgia to kick you in the teeth. This is where you go when you're 200 miles away from a town you thought you'd never want to return to but suddenly you're pining for it.

Amanda and Zach grew up 30 miles from each other and met as adults through poetry. Explore both the male and female perspective of what it's like to grow up hemmed in by an area's economic struggle. These poems mine through life, love, longing and death, they're for home and away, and the inner strength that is not deterred by any of those things.

SPLIT BOOK #1

What are Split Books?

Two full-length books from two poets in one + there's a collaborative split between the poets in the middle!

COLLECT THEM ALL!

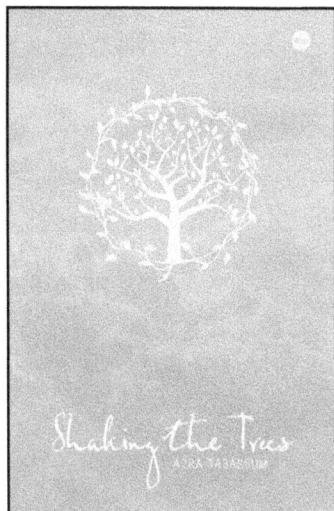

SHAKING THE TREES
Poetry by Azra Tabassum

| $12 | 72 pages | 5.5" x 8.5" | softcover |

ISBN: 978-0692232408

From the very first page *Shaking the Trees* meets you at the edge of the forest, extends a limb & seduces you into taking a walk through the dark & light of connection. Suddenly, like a gunshot in the very-near distance, you find yourself traipsing though a full-blown love story that you can't find your way out of because the story is actually the landscape underneath your feet. It's okay though, you won't get lost– you won't go hungry. Azra shakes every tree along the way so their fruit blankets the ground before you. She picks up pieces & hands them to you but not before she shows you how she can love you so gently it will feel like she's unpeeling you carefully from yourself. She tells you that it isn't about the bite but the warm juice that slips from the lips down chin. She holds your hand when you're trudging through the messier parts, shoes getting stuck in the muck of it all, but you'll keep going with the pulp of the fruit still stuck in-between your teeth, the juice will dry in the crooks of your elbows & in the lines on your palms. You'll taste bittersweet for days.

"I honestly haven't read a collection like this before, or at least I can't remember having read one. My heart was wrecked by Azra. It's like that opening line in Fahrenheit 451 when Bradbury says, "It was a pleasure to burn." It really was a pleasure being wrecked by it."

— **NOURA**
of *NouraReads*

"I wanted to cry and cheer and fuck. I wanted to take the next person I saw and kiss them straight on the lips and say, "Remember this moment for the rest of your life."

— **CHELSEA MILLER**

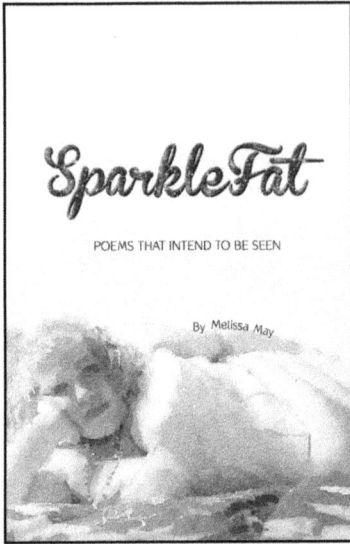

POEMS THAT INTEND TO BE SEEN

By Melissa May

SPARKLEFAT
Poetry by Melissa May

| $12 | 62 pages | 5.5" x 8.5" | softcover |

SparkleFat is a loud, unapologetic, intentional book of poetry about my body, about your body, about fat bodies and how they move through the world in every bit of their flash and spark and burst. Some of the poems are painful, some are raucous celebrations, some are reminders and love letters and quiet gifts back to the vessel that has traveled me so gracefully - some are a hymnal of yes, but all of them sparkle. All of them don't mind if you look – really. They built their own house of intention, and they draped that shit in lime green sequins. All of them intend to be seen. All of them have no more fucks to give about a world that wants them to be quiet.

"I didn't know how much I needed this book until I found myself, three pages in, ugly crying on the plane next to a concerned looking business man. This book is the most glorious, glittery pink permission slip. It made me want to go on a scavenger hunt for every speck of shame in my body and sing hot, sweaty R&B songs to it. There is no voice more authentic, generous and resounding than Melissa May. From her writing, to her performance, to her role in the community she delivers fierce integrity & staggering passion. From the first time I watched her nervously step to the mic, to the last time she crushed me in a slam, it is has been an honor to watch her astound the poetry slam world and inspire us all to be not just better writers but better people. We need her."

— LAUREN ZUNIGA
Author of *The Smell of Good Mud*

"*SparkleFat* is a firework display of un-shame. Melissa May's work celebrates all of the things we have been so long told deserved no streamers. This collection invites every fat body out to the dance and steams up the windows in the backseat of the car afterwards by kissing the spots we thought (or even hoped) no one noticed but are deserving of love just the same as our mouths."

— RACHEL WILEY
Author of *Fat Girl Finishing School*

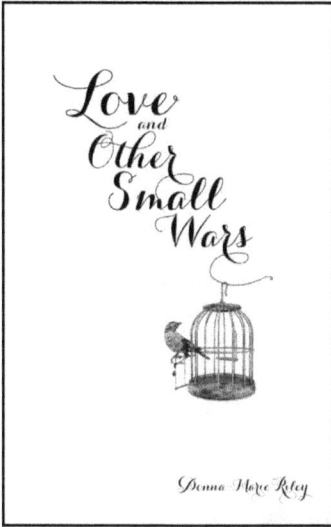

LOVE AND OTHER SMALL WARS

Poetry by Donna-Marie Riley

| $12 | 76 pages | 5.5" x 8.5" | softcover |

ISBN: 978-0615931111

Love and Other Small Wars reminds us that when you come back from combat usually the most fatal of wounds are not visible. Riley's debut collection is an arsenal of deeply personal poems that embody an intensity that is truly impressive yet their hands are tender. She enlists you. She gives you camouflage & a pair of boots so you can stay the course through the minefield of her heart. You will track the lovely flow of her soft yet fierce voice through a jungle of powerful imagery on womanhood, relationships, family, grief, sexuality & love, amidst other matters. Battles with the heart aren't easily won but Riley hits every mark. You'll be relieved that you're on the same side. Much like war, you'll come back from this book changed.

"Riley's work is wise, intense, affecting, and uniquely crafted. This collection illuminates her ability to write with both a gentle hand and a bold spirit. She inspires her readers and creates an indelible need inside of them to consume more of her exceptional poetry. I could read *Love and Other Small Wars* all day long…and I did."

— **APRIL MICHELLE BRATTEN**
editor of *Up the Staircase Quarterly*

"Riley's poems are personal, lyrical and so vibrant they practically leap off the page, which also makes them terrifying at times. A beautiful debut."

— **BIANCA STEWART**

Other titles available from
WORDS DANCE PUBLISHING

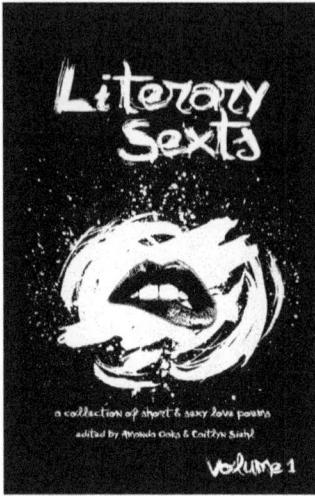

LITERARY SEXTS

A Collection of Short & Sexy Love Poems
(Volume 1)

| $12 | 42 pages | 5.5" x 8.5" | softcover |

ISBN: 978-0615959726

Literary Sexts is a modern day anthology of short love poems with subtle erotic undertones edited by Amanda Oaks & Caitlyn Siehl. Hovering around 50 contributors & 124 poems, this book reads is like one long & very intense conversation between two lovers. It's absolutely breathtaking. These are poems that you would text to your lover. Poems that you would slip into a back pocket, suitcase, wallet or purse on the sly. Poems that you would write on slips of paper & stick under your crush's windshield wiper. Poems that you would write on a Post-it note & leave on the bathroom mirror.

**HIT #1
ON AMAZON'S
HOT NEW
RELEASE LIST!**

"It's like 100+ new ways to make a reader blush. The imagery is so subtle yet completely thrilling..." **NOW I NEED A COLD SHOWER!"**
                                                    - K. W.

"**I DEVOURED IT!** I physically wanted to eat these poems. I wanted to wear them on my skin like perfume..."
                                                    - A. G.

"I have consumed this in ways that have left my insides looking like strips of velvet fabric... **SO ORGASMIC!"**
                                                    - K. B.

"**A MAELSTROM OF EMOTIONS!** I only hope that there is a Volume 2, a Volume 3 and so on because I need more of this!"
                                                    - Daniel CZ

Unrequited love? We've all been there.

Enter:

WHAT TO DO AFTER SHE SAYS NO
by Kris Ryan.

This skillfully designed 10-part poem explores what it's like to ache for someone. This is the book you buy yourself or a friend when you are going through a breakup or a one-sided crush, it's the perfect balance between aha, humor & heartbreak.

WHAT TO DO AFTER SHE SAYS NO
A Poem by Kris Ryan

$10 | 104 pages | 5" x 8" | softcover | ISBN: 978-0615870045

"*What to Do After She Says No* takes us from Shanghai to the interior of a refrigerator, but mostly dwells inside the injured human heart, exploring the aftermath of emotional betrayal. This poem is a compact blast of brutality, with such instructions as "Climb onto the roof and jump off. If you break your leg, you are awake. If you land without injury, pinch and twist at your arm until you wake up." Ryan's use of the imperative often leads us to a reality where pain is the only outcome, but this piece is not without tenderness, and certainly not without play, with sounds and images ricocheting off each other throughout. Anticipate the poetry you wish you knew about during your last bad breakup; this poem offers a first "foothold to climb out" from that universal experience."

— LISA MANGINI

"Reading Kris Ryan's *What To Do After She Says No* is like watching your heart pound outside of your chest. Both an unsettling visual experience and a hurricane of sadness and rebirth—this book demands more than just your attention, it takes a little bit of your soul, and in the end, makes everything feel whole again."

— JOHN DORSEY
author of ***Tombstone Factory***

"*What to Do After She Says No* is exquisite. Truly, perfectly exquisite. It pulls you in on a familiar and wild ride of a heart blown open and a mind twisting in an effort to figure it all out. It's raw and vibrant...and in the same breath comforting. I want to crawl inside this book and live in a world where heartache is expressed so magnificently.

— JO ANNA ROTHMAN
MA, Coach & Conjurer of Electric Creative Wholeness

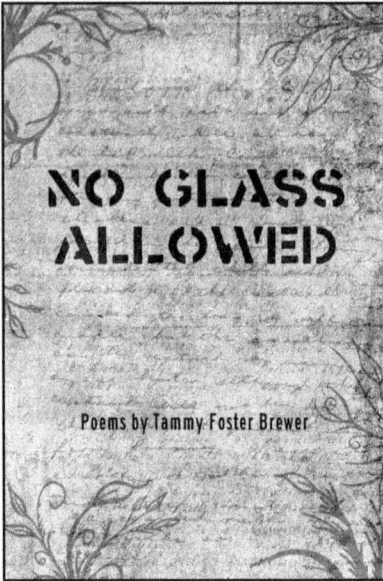

Tammy Foster Brewer is the type of poet who makes me wish I could write poetry instead of novels. From motherhood to love to work, Tammy's poems highlight the extraordinary in the ordinary and leave the reader wondering how he did not notice what was underneath all along. I first heard Tammy read 'The Problem is with Semantics' months ago, and it's stayed with me ever since. Now that I've read the entire collection, I only hope I can make room to keep every one of her poems in my heart and mind tomorrow and beyond.

— **NICOLE ROSS,** author

NO GLASS ALLOWED
Poetry by Tammy Foster Brewer

$12 | 56 pages | 6" x 9" | softcover | ISBN: 978-0615870007

Brewer's collection is filled with uncanny details that readers will wear like the accessories of womanhood. Fishing the Chattahoochee, sideways trees, pollen on a car, white dresses and breast milk, and so much more -- all parts of a deeply intellectual pondering of what is often painful and human regarding the other halves of mothers and daughters, husbands and wives, lovers and lost lovers, children and parents.

— **NICHOLAS BELARDES**
author of *Songs of the Glue Machines*

Tammy deftly juxtaposes distinct imagery with stories that seem to collide in her brilliant poetic mind. Stories of transmissions and trees and the words we utter, or don't. Of floods and forgiveness, conversations and car lanes, bread and beginnings, awe and expectations, desire and leaps of faith that leave one breathless, and renewed.

"When I say I am a poet / I mean my house has many windows" has to be one of the best descriptions of what it's like to be a contemporary female poet who not only holds down a day job and raises a family, but whose mind and heart regularly file away fleeting images and ideas that might later be woven into something permanent, and perhaps even beautiful. This ability is not easily acquired. It takes effort, and time, and the type of determination only some writers, like Tammy, possess and are willing to actively exercise.

— **KAREN DEGROOT CARTER**
author of *One Sister's Song*

WORDS DANCE PUBLISHING

DO YOU WRITE POETRY?
Submit it to our biweekly online magazine!

We publish poems every Tuesday & Thursday on website.

Come see what all the fuss is about!

We like Poems that sneak up on you. Poems that make out with you. Poems that bloody your mouth just to kiss it clean. Poems that bite your cheek so you spend all day tonguing the wound. Poems that vandalize your heart. Poems that act like a tin can phone connecting you to your childhood. Fire Alarm Poems. Glitterbomb Poems. Jailbreak Poems. Poems that could marry the land or the sea; that are both the hero & the villain. Poems that are the matches when there is a city-wide power outage. Poems that throw you overboard just dive in & save your ass. Poems that push you down on the stoop in front of history's door screaming at you to knock. Poems that are soft enough to fall asleep on. Poems that will still be clinging to the walls inside of your bones on your 90th birthday. We like poems. Submit yours.

WORDSDANCE.COM

www.ingramcontent.com/pod-product-compliance
Lightning Source LLC
Chambersburg PA
CBHW022012090426

42741CB00007B/998